Sea Urchins

Tori Miller

PowerKiDS
press

New York

To my son David, who really did step on a sea urchin

Published in 2009 by The Rosen Publishing Group, Inc.
29 East 21st Street, New York, NY 10010

First Edition

Editor: Joanne Randolph
Book Design: Greg Tucker
Photo Researcher: Jessica Gerweck

Photo Credits: Cover © Marevision/Age Fotostock; pp. 5, 7, 15 Shutterstock.com; p. 9 © George Grail/Getty Images; p. 11 © Georgette Douwma/Getty Images; pp. 12–13 © Juan Carlos Calvin/Age Fotostock; p. 17 © Brandon Cole/Getty Images; p. 19 © Paul Nicklen/Getty Images; p. 21 © Wim van Egmond/Getty Images.

Library of Congress Cataloging-in-Publication Data

Miller, Tori.
  Sea urchins / Tori Miller. — 1st. ed.
    p. cm. — (Freaky fish)
  ISBN 978-1-4358-2756-1 (library binding) — ISBN 978-1-4358-3173-5 (pbk.)
ISBN 978-1-4358-3179-7 (6-pack)
  1. Sea urchins—Juvenile literature. I. Title.
  QL384.E2M55 2009
  593.9'5—dc22
                                2008033910

Manufactured in the United States of America

Contents

Trouble at the Beach!

Have you ever looked into a tide pool? You might see crabs and little fish. There is probably seaweed, too. There might be something else there that you may not see right away. Be careful around tide pools since they are often home to sea urchins. You do not want to step on one!

Sea urchins look a little like pincushions, with sharp **spines** sticking out all over their bodies. Sea urchins are fun to look at, but you do not want to touch them. Those sharp spines can hurt. Let's learn a little more about these pincushions of the sea!

This sea urchin sits in the water of the Red Sea, which is between western Asia and northeastern Africa. You can see the sharp spines all over the sea urchin's body.

Underwater Hedgehogs

There are about 800 different **species** of sea urchin. Sea urchins are sometimes called sea hedgehogs because their round, spiny bodies make them look like hedgehogs. Hedgehogs are small land animals that have sharp spines on their backs. Most sea urchins are dark in color. They are commonly black, reddish brown, dark green, or dark purple.

The smallest sea urchins are only .5 inch (1 cm) across, about the size of your thumbnail! The largest ones can grow to be 1.5 feet (46 cm) across. Most sea urchins are about the size of your hand.

These sea urchins have long blue spines. Their bodies are not that big, but the long spines make them seem much bigger.

Sea Urchins at Home

Sea urchins live in most of the warmer oceans of the world. There are many different kinds of sea urchins in the Indian Ocean around Southeast Asia. There are also sea urchins in the Atlantic Ocean and Pacific Ocean.

Some sea urchins can be found in deep water, but most sea urchins like shallow water, or water that is not deep. They live on the bottom of the ocean and can often be found in tide pools. Some species live among the rocks, while others can bury themselves in the sand. If you are playing in the ocean where sea urchins live, be sure to watch where you step!

These purple sea urchins are living in a tide pool in Washington. Purple sea urchins are known to live off the west coast of North America from Canada to the Baja Peninsula.

Spines!

Sea urchins have round shells that cover the soft parts inside their bodies. A sea urchin shell is called a test. A sea urchin's spines stick out of its test.

Sea urchins have many sharp spines. In some species, they can be up to 1 foot (30 cm) long! Species that hide in the rocks or sand tend to have shorter spines. Sea urchins can move their spines to point them at an enemy. They can also fix their spines in place. The ends of the spines break off easily. A **predator** that tries to eat a sea urchin may find itself with a mouthful of spines! That hurts!

This is a red sea urchin, which is known for its long, movable spines. Its spines grow from the test in groups, with five parts in between each grouping that are free from spines.

The Sea Urchin:
Freaky Facts

- People in Korea and Japan eat parts of the sea urchin.

- Some sea urchins can live up to 100 years!

- The **tube feet** on a sea urchin take in air from the water.

- Sea urchins are related to sand dollars.

- Some sea urchins use their spines to help them walk.

- Some sea urchins are **poisonous**.

- Some animals, such as cardinal fish, swim near sea urchins and use the urchins' spines to keep themselves safe.

○ A single sea urchin can produce 20 million eggs! That is a lot of eggs.

○ Sea urchins and people have more than 7,000 **genes** in common.

○ Sea urchins do not have ears or eyes, but they do have the genes that people have for sight and hearing.

Five Teeth and Lots of Feet

A sea urchin is not just a big ball of spines. A sea urchin also has five rows of small pairs of feet called tube feet. The tube feet come from tiny holes in the test. Sea urchins use their tube feet to walk and climb. Most sea urchins have suckers at the ends of their tube feet to help them move and hold on to rocks.

A sea urchin has a mouth on its underside. The mouth has five platelike teeth that are in a circle. The name for a sea urchin's mouth is Aristotle's lantern. It got this name from one of the first people to describe a sea urchin's mouth. Aristotle was a Greek teacher who lived over 2,000 years ago. He said the sea urchin's mouth looked like a horn lantern, which was a five-sided lamp commonly used in his time.

You can clearly see the sea urchin's mouth in this picture. The five teeth are used to scrape food from rocks and to crush the shells of small sea animals.

Scraping Up a Meal

Most sea urchins eat **algae**, seaweed, and small dead animals. They generally eat by scraping, or shaving, their food off rocks with their teeth. This is commonly called rasping. Some sea urchins eat plants and small animals that they find in the sand.

Sea urchins also eat food they find on their bodies. In addition to spines, sea urchins have **pincers** near their mouths. They use their pincers to clean themselves. Often they find bits of plants and small animals stuck in their spines. The pincers pass these bits of food to the mouth.

This sea urchin moves slowly along the rock and eats the algae and barnacles that cover the rock here. The animals on its back are not food but are used to help the sea urchin hide.

Sea Urchin Enemies

Baby sea urchins are food for many underwater predators, from tiny fish called wrasse to giant whales. Once sea urchins are full grown, they have fewer predators, since most animals do not want a mouthful of spines. However, some predators have found ways to deal with the spines. A sea otter will grab a sea urchin from the ocean floor. Then the otter will float on its back and use a rock to crack open the hard shell and get to the soft insides.

Seagulls also like to eat sea urchins. They deal with the hard shells by plucking the sea urchins out of the water with their beaks, or bills, and then dropping them on the hard rocks.

A sea star is shown here making a feast out of a sea urchin. It grabs the urchin with its arms and then pushes out its stomach from inside its body to eat the sea urchin.

A Sea Urchin's Life

Like most living things, sea urchins come together to make new sea urchins. Female sea urchins put millions of eggs into the water. The eggs are **fertilized** as they float there. The eggs open quickly, and **larvae** come out. Sea urchin larvae look very different from adult sea urchins. They look like arrows, with their two long arms used for swimming and their mouth in the middle.

After about a month, the larvae's arms shorten and they grow spines and tube legs. At this point, the sea urchin sinks to the bottom of the ocean and begins life as an adult.

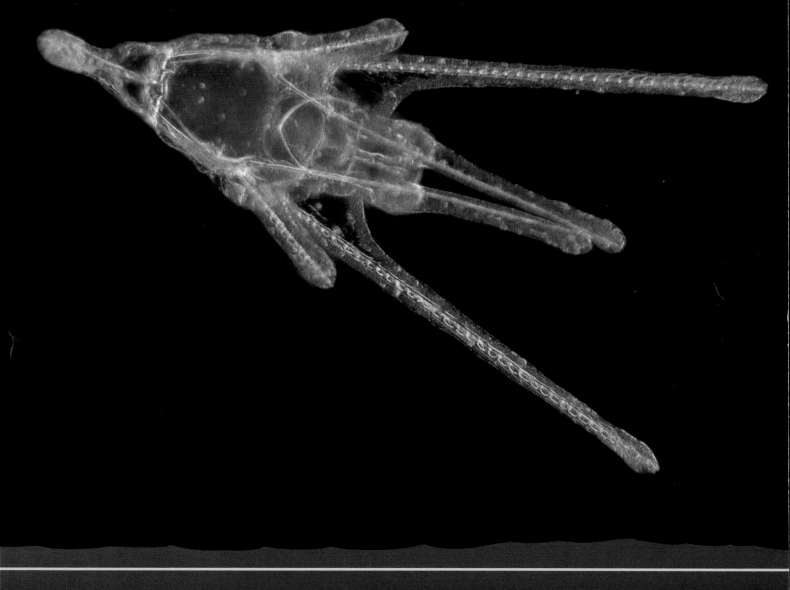

This is a sea urchin larva, also called a pluteus. The sea urchin spends several weeks in the tiny pluteus stage before it changes into its adult form.

Our Cousins the Sea Urchins

Did you know that you are related to the sea urchin? **Scientists** have discovered that sea urchins have a lot in common with people! Even though sea urchins do not look like us, they have many of the same genes that we do.

Scientists have also discovered that sea urchins can fight illness much better than people can. They believe that by studying the sea urchin, they can find ways to help people with illnesses, such as cancer, **Alzheimer's disease**, and **Parkinson's disease**. Sea urchins are an important part of the web of life that makes up our world.

Glossary

algae (AL-jee) Plantlike living things without roots or stems that live in water.

Alzheimer's disease (ALTS-hy-merz dih-ZEEZ) An illness that causes problems with the mind, such as extreme forgetfulness.

fertilized (FUR-tuh-lyzd) Male cells put inside an egg to make babies.

genes (JEENZ) Many tiny parts in the center of a cell. Your genes tell your cells how your body will look and act.

larvae (LAHR-vee) Animals in the early life period in which they have a wormlike form.

Parkinson's disease (PAR-kin-sinz dih-ZEEZ) An illness that causes people to shake and to have a hard time speaking.

pincers (PIN-surz) Sharp claws.

poisonous (POYZ-nus) Causing pain or death.

predator (PREH-duh-ter) An animal that kills other animals for food.

scientists (SY-un-tists) People who study the world.

species (SPEE-sheez) A single kind of living thing. All people are one species.

spines (SPYNZ) Sharp, pointy things.

tube feet (TOOB FEET) Water-filled, strawlike parts on some sea animals that are used for moving.

Index

Web Sites

Due to the changing nature of Internet links, PowerKids Press has developed an online list of Web sites related to the subject of this book. This site is updated regularly. Please use this link to access the list:
www.powerkidslinks.com/ffish/urchin/